KU-515-825

Bromley Libraries

30128 80160 593 5

I ♥ Craft

TOYS

Rita Storey

FRANKLIN WATTS
LONDON·SYDNEY

First published in 2014 by
Franklin Watts
338 Euston Road
London NW1 3BH

Franklin Watts Australia
Level 17/207 Kent Street
Sydney NSW 2000

Copyright © Franklin Watts 2014
All rights reserved.

Packaged for Franklin Watts by Storeybooks
rita@storeybooks.co.uk
Designer: Rita Storey
Editor: Sarah Ridley
Crafts made by: Rita Storey
Series editor: Sarah Peutrill
Photography: Tudor Photography, Banbury
www.tudorphotography.co.uk

A CIP catalogue record for this book is available
from the British Library.

Printed in China

Dewey classification: 746.4'32'043

ISBN (hardback): 978 1 4451 3073 6
ISBN (library ebook): 978 1 4451 3074 3

Cover images: Tudor Photography, Banbury

Franklin Watts is a division of Hachette Children's Books,
an Hachette UK company
www.hachette.co.uk

Before you start

Some of the projects in this book require scissors, paint, strong
glue, pins, a compass or a sewing needle. When using these
things we would recommend that children are supervised by
a responsible adult.
Please note: keep homemade toys and products
away from babies and small children.
They cannot be tested for safety.

Contents

Pom-pom Pets

Pom-pom dogs and cats make purr-fect pets. They live happily in your pocket until it is time to play.

To make a pom-pom dog you will need:

* pencil
* thin white paper
* scissors
* 4 sewing pins
* brown felt * black felt
* paintbrush
* glue
* 8cm pom-pom made from cream wool (see pages 26 – 27)
* 2 googly eyes

1 Trace the dog templates on page 28 onto white paper. Cut them out.

2 Pin the ear and nose templates onto black felt and the muzzle template onto brown felt. Cut each one out. Remove the pins and templates.

3 Using the paintbrush, put a dab of glue onto one side of each shape. Glue the shapes onto the pom-pom as shown in the picture above. Glue on the googly eyes either side of the nose.

4 Glue along the straight side of each felt ear. Glue the ears onto the pom-pom on each side of the head at the top.

To make a pom-pom cat you will need:

* pencil

* thin white paper

* scissors   * 4 sewing pins

* black felt

* white felt

* pink felt

* paintbrush   * glue

* 8cm pom-pom made from black wool (see pages 26 – 27)

* 2 googly eyes

* tapestry needle

* small amount of white wool

1 Trace the cat templates on page 28 onto white paper. Cut them out. Pin the ear templates onto black felt, the muzzle template onto white felt and the nose template onto pink felt. Cut each one out. Remove the pins and templates.

2 Using the paintbrush, put a dab of glue onto one side of the muzzle and nose. Glue the muzzle halfway down the pom-pom. Glue the nose at the top of the muzzle.

3 Glue a googly eye either side of the nose.

4 Paint glue along one side of each ear. Tuck the glued part of the ear into the pom-pom just above the eye on each side of the head.

5 Thread the needle with white wool. Pull the doubled wool through the muzzle under the nose. Cut through the loop of wool to release the needle.

5

Big Blue Robot

Robots are machines which can be programmed to do all sorts of jobs. This big blue robot is waiting for your instructions.

You will need:

* balloon
* piece of thin card 19mm x 30mm
* masking tape
* newspaper torn into small pieces
* paintbrushes
* white glue mixed with water
* blue paint
* 2 small cardboard tubes
* 2 pieces of thin card 9cm x 4cm
* strong glue * silver tape
* scissors * kitchen towel
* 2 red pipe cleaners
* yellow pipe cleaner
* 3 drawing pins * plastic nozzle from a paint bottle
* 2 small plastic containers
* black paint
* bits and pieces to decorate the robot (see owl opposite)

1 Blow up the balloon and tie the end. With the long side at the bottom, make the bigger piece of thin card into a tube so that it fits around the balloon. Tape the edges of the card together with masking tape.

2 Paint the pieces of newspaper with glue on both sides and paste them all over the balloon and the cardboard tube. Continue until you have covered the whole shape with two layers of overlapping pieces of paper. This is called papier-mâché. Leave to dry.

3 Paint the shape with blue paint. Leave to dry.

4 Paint the cardboard tubes with blue paint. Leave to dry.

5 Cover both sides of the small pieces of thin card with silver tape. Trim off any overlapping tape.

6 Bend each piece of card as shown above. Glue them inside the end of each cardboard tube. Decorate the ends of the tubes with more silver tape.

7 Scrunch some kitchen towel into the other end of each cardboard tube. Using masking tape, tape in place. Paint the tape blue and leave to dry.

8 With the rounded end at the top, glue a tube onto each side of the robot.

9 Twist the red and yellow pipe cleaners around the end of the paintbrush. Push one end of each red pipe cleaner into the nozzle. Glue the bottom of the nozzle onto the top of the robot. Attach the yellow pipe cleaner to the side of the robot with the drawing pins, as shown in the photo.

10 Paint the plastic containers with black paint. Leave to dry. Glue onto the bottom of the robot to form feet. Glue on the extra decorations.

Look in the recycling bin to find bits and pieces to decorate your robot. This robot is decorated with the plastic cover from some batteries, and the lids from small jars.

Mini Kite

This colourful little kite will fly brilliantly even in the lightest of winds.

You will need:

* A4 sheet of thin green card
* pencil
* ruler
* stapler
* hole punch
* clear sticky tape
* drinking straw
* 3 metres of thin string
* lolly stick
* brightly coloured plastic carrier bag
* scissors * masking tape
* circles of thin coloured paper in different sizes
* white glue and spreader

You can decorate your kite with glitter glue to add extra sparkle. Go easy though or the kite will be too heavy to fly.

1 Fold the sheet of green card in half along the longest side.

2 At the bottom of the card, use the ruler to measure 6cm from the folded edge. Mark the point with the pencil.

At the top of the card, measure 1.5cm from the folded edge. Mark the point with the pencil. Using a pencil and a ruler, draw a line to join up the two marks.

3 Lay the ruler along the line you have just drawn. Bend the card along the line and over the ruler to make a flap. Take out the ruler. Crease the fold with your fingernail.

4 Bend the flap back. Staple just under the pencil line.

5 Use the hole punch to make a hole approximately 7cm from the narrow end of the flap. Open out the card to form the body of the kite.

6 Using clear tape, fix the straw onto the top of the kite as shown. Make sure that both ends of the straw touch the edges of the back of the kite (see the photograph above).

7 Tie one end of the string through the hole in the kite's flap and knot it. Tape the other end of the string to the lolly stick. Wind two metres of string around the stick.

8 Roll up the carrier bag from the opening to the base. Using scissors, cut two pieces, 2cm wide, from the roll. Open out the pieces.

9 Using masking tape, attach the strips of plastic to the narrow end of the kite at the back. Glue the circles of paper onto the front of the kite to decorate it.

Go fly your kite outside!

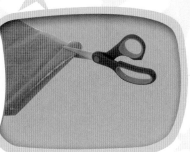

Skittles

T urn some plastic bottles into a funky set of skittles to use with friends.

To make a set of skittles you will need:

* 6 x 500ml clean, empty plastic drinks bottles with their lids
* plastic funnel
* 300g fine sand
* white glue mixed with the same amount of water
* 1 sheet each of six different colours of tissue paper
* poster paints * paintbrush
* tennis ball (to play the game)

To make a scorecard you will need:

* A4 sheet of paper cut into 4 equal strips (74.25mm x 210mm)
* strip of card slightly larger than a paper strip
* stapler * ruler
* felt-tip pen

1 Take the lid off one of the bottles. Using the funnel, pour 50g of fine sand into the bottle. Put the lid back on. Screw up tightly. Repeat with the other five bottles.

2 Tear a sheet of tissue paper into pieces. Paint some of the glue mixture onto the bottle and stick on the tissue paper, overlapping the pieces as shown.

3 Continue until the bottle and lid are covered with tissue paper. Leave to dry. Repeat with the remaining five bottles using a different colour of tissue paper for each.

4 Using poster paint, create a design on each bottle (see photo below for ideas). Leave to dry.

5 Place the strips of paper on top of the card, as shown in the photograph, and staple them together. Draw two columns on the paper using the ruler and felt-tip pen. Write in each player's name. Keep score as you play the game.

Name	Score
Luke	||| ||||
Total	1 3

How to play

Put a marker on the floor where each player will stand.

The first player stands behind the marker and rolls the ball at the skittles. For every skittle knocked down the player scores one point, marked on the scorecard with a line. If all the skittles are knocked down they are put back up for the next throw. The player has three rolls, one after the other.

The next player takes their turn. After three rolls the next player has their turn, and so on.

To find the winner, add up the score for each player.

Ask a grown up where you can play the game.

11

Monster Truck

Get ready for some monster fun with this super cool truck.

You will need:

* 4 x 2-litre clean, empty plastic drinks bottles with their lids
* scissors * ruler
* clear sticky tape
* black paint
* roll of silver duct tape
* cardboard tube * lolly stick
* small box (approx. 7cm x 8cm x 3cm)
* medium-sized box (approx 14cm x 8cm x 4cm)
* masking tape
* blue paint * paintbrush
* 2 x red pipe cleaners
* pencil * glue
* 4 x circles of thin yellow card
* 4 x circles of thin blue card
* flames cut from red and yellow card (use the template on page 28)
* 2 x bottle tops painted silver with a circle of yellow card glued onto the centre

1 Ask an adult to cut the bottles in half. Now make a mark, 7cm from the bottom of each half bottle. Using scissors, cut the bottom 7cm off each half bottle. Trim the top of each half bottle to approximately 5cm in length.

2 Push a top section into a bottom section to make a small bottle (see picture above). Use the sticky tape to join the two sections together. Repeat with the other three bottles.

3 Remove the lids from the mini bottles. Pour a little black paint into each bottle.

4 Screw the lids back onto the bottles very tightly. Ask an adult to check that the tape is secure and the lid is on tightly. Shake each bottle until the paint covers all of the inside.

5 Take off the lids. Leave the bottles to dry. Put the lids back on. Using duct tape, tape the lids of the bottles together in pairs (see picture above).

6 Cut a section of the card tube. Wrap it around the bottle-top axle. Tape it together loosely so that it turns freely.

7 Lay the lolly stick onto the duct tape as shown in the picture above.

8 Wrap the duct tape around the bottle-top axles to join the pairs of bottles together.

9 Open one end of the small box. Cut out a triangle shape as shown, to create the windscreen. Using masking tape, tape the box closed.

10 Tape the small box onto the top of the bigger box. Paint the boxes blue. Leave them to dry. Cut pieces of silver duct tape and stick them on the painted box to make windows.

11 Curl the ends of the pipe cleaners around the pencil. Leave 4cm of the middle sections uncurled. Glue the uncurled middle sections to the base of the bigger box. Leave to dry.

12 Curl the pipe cleaners around the bottle-top axles. Glue the circles of blue card onto the yellow ones. Glue a yellow card circle onto the centre of each wheel. Glue the flames onto both sides of the truck. Glue the bottle tops onto the front of the truck.

You are ready to roll!

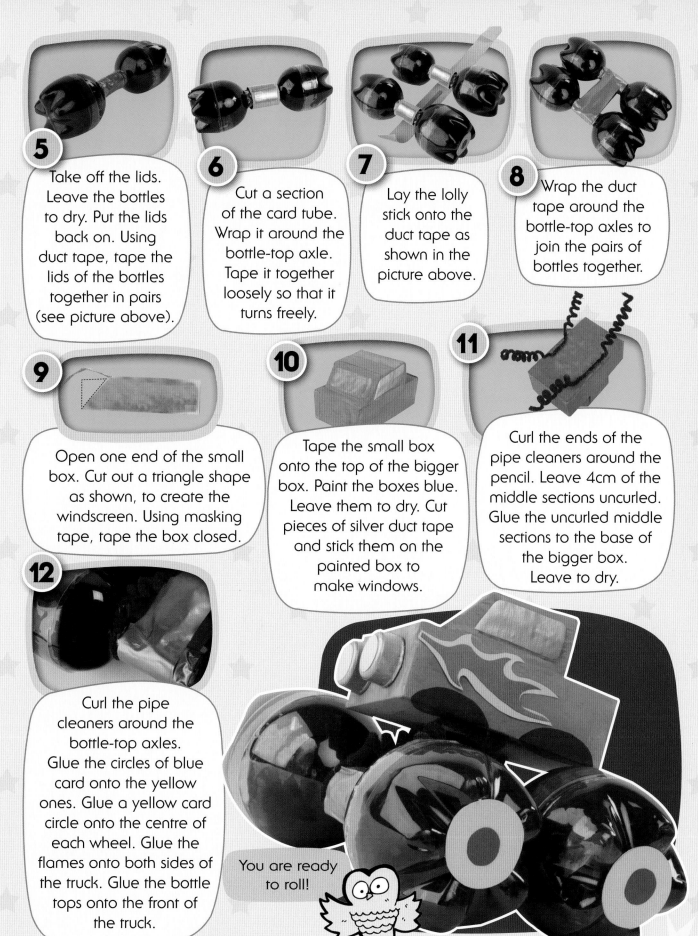

13

Dolls' House

Give your dolls a smart new home in this pretty dolls' house.

You will need:

* 2 cardboard shoe boxes 17cm x 30cm x 10cm
* paintbrush
* white paint
* double-sided tape
* wrapping paper
* A3 sheet of cream card
* A3 sheet of red paper
* glue and spreader
* pencil * scissors
* red, yellow, blue and green felt-tip pens
* 3 x 3cm x 2cm pieces of duct tape

You can download the windows and door from www.franklinwatts.co.uk and glue them onto the front of the house.

1 Paint the inside of each shoe box white. Leave to dry.

2 Using double-sided tape, join the two boxes, one on top of the other.

3 Cover the back of the boxes with wrapping paper.

2cm 4cm

2cm

4cm

1cm

4 Lay the joined boxes on top of the cream card and draw around them. Remove the boxes. Use a ruler and pencil to draw a line 4cm taller than the outline of the boxes and 2cm wider at each side. Cut out pieces from both sides of the card, as shown above.

14

5 Lay the house-shaped card on the red paper as shown. Draw around the roof shape with the pencil. Take the card away and cut along the line on the red paper.

6 Glue the red paper roof onto the top of the house-shaped card.

7 Use the template on page 30 to trace six window shapes and one door onto thin white paper. Colour them in with felt-tip pens.

9 Using felt-tip pens, draw a design of flowers and leaves to decorate the front of the dolls' house.

8 Cut out the shapes. Glue them onto the front of the dolls' house.

11 Stick the over-lapping pieces of tape to the back of the house front to make three hinges. It should look like the picture below from the top,

10 Attach three pieces of duct tape onto the right-hand side of the side of the box, as shown in the picture above.

Who will live in this new home?

15

Target Board

Aim to win with a star score on this colourful target board game.

You will need:

* piece of foam board or cardboard, 38cm square
* ruler * pencil
* drawing pin
* 2 pieces of string 25cm long
* craft knife – ask an adult to use it
* piece of orange felt, 38cm square
* glue * paintbrush
* piece of green felt, 30cm square
* piece of purple felt, 20cm square
* piece of orange felt, 10cm square
* piece of green felt, 10cm square
* circular objects to draw around approximately 30cm, 20cm and 10cm in diameter
* scissors * tracing paper
* sewing pin
* scraps of yellow and pink felt
* 6cm length of sticky-backed velcro
* sticky tape
* 3 practice golf balls

1 Draw a line from the top corner of the foam board to the opposite corner on the bottom edge. Draw a line between the other two corners.

2 Push a drawing pin into the point where the two lines meet. Make a loop in one of the pieces of string. Put the loop over the drawing pin. Tie the pencil onto the other end of the string so that it is just on the edge of the card.

Hold the string taut and draw a circle that fits the full size of the card.

Ask an adult to cut out the circle with the craft knife.

3 Place the circle of board onto the large piece of orange felt. Draw around the circle. Cut along the line. Using the paintbrush, paint glue onto one side of the felt. Press the glued side onto the circle of board.

4 Draw around the circular objects and cut out felt circles from the 30cm (green), 20cm (purple) and 10cm (orange) felt squares. Paint the circles with glue and stick them onto the base as shown above and in the main photograph below.

5 Trace the star template on page 31 onto tracing paper. Pin the tracing paper star onto the remaining piece of green felt and cut it out. Take off the pin and template. Glue the star into position in the centre of the small orange circle.

6 Trace the number templates on page 30 onto tracing paper. Pin each template onto a scrap of felt and cut it out. Take off the pin and template. Glue the felt numbers onto the board as shown in the main photo below.

7 Cut the velcro into six 1cm pieces. Peel off the backing. Stick two pieces onto each practice golf ball.

8 Tape the remaining piece of string onto the back of the board. Use the string to hang the board up.

How to play

Put a marker on the floor where each player will stand.

Gently throw the balls at the board.

Add up your score.

The player with the highest score is the winner.

Who will score the highest?

Puppet Theatre

Put on a great puppet show in your very own puppet theatre.

You will need:

* cardboard box approximately 28cm x 20cm x 30cm
* scissors * paintbrush
* red poster paint
* duct tape * glue and spreader
* A3 sheet of blue paper
* A4 sheet of yellow paper
* A4 sheet of thin white paper
* A4 sheet of pink paper
* felt-tip pens * striped fabric
* stapler

1 Open out the cardboard box and cut off the top flaps. Cut off one side. Cut a square out of the middle panel.

2 Paint the inside and outside of the box red.

3 Pull the sides towards each other so that they are at an angle to the middle panel. Tape them in place.

4 Copy the template shapes on page 29 onto the blue and yellow sheets of paper. Cut them out. Glue onto the theatre as shown in the photograph on page 19.

5 Copy or trace the masks on page 29 onto thin white paper. Colour in the masks with felt-tip pens. Leave to dry.

6 Cut out the masks and glue them into the centre of the middle panel.

7 Copy or trace the stars onto yellow and pink paper. Cut them out and glue them onto each side of the stage.

8 To create stage curtains, cut two pieces of fabric so that they are half the width of the stage and a bit longer than the height. Fold each piece of fabric in half. Make some small folds along the top edge. Staple the folds in place.

9 With the folded edge at the top, use duct tape to attach the curtains to either side of the stage opening.

Learn how to make a sock puppet (pages 20 – 21) or a hand puppet (pages 22 – 23) to put on a show in your theatre.

Sock Puppet

This cute little puppet can tell great jokes with a little help from you!

You will need:

* A4 piece of card
* red felt
* pencil * biro
* scissors
* clean purple sock
* wadding
* glue
* glue spreader
* 2 metres of yellow wool
* tapestry needle
* 2 large buttons
* piece of card 6cm x 3cm
* 2cm purple pom-pom from a craft shop

1 Use the template on page 31 to cut the shape shown above from the piece of card.

2 Draw around the card onto the red felt. Cut out the shape.

3 Fold the card in half. Open it out again.

4 Slide the card into the sock, right down to the toe. Push the clump of wadding into the toe of the sock, above the card.

5 Turn the sock over. Spread glue onto the red felt shape. Glue it onto the outside of the sock to line up with the card inside. The glue will soak through to the card. Leave to dry.

6 Turn the sock over again. Cut a 20-cm length of yellow wool. Thread the needle with the wool. Tie a knot in the end. Use the wool to sew a button onto the side of the sock above the wadding. Do the same with the other button on the opposite side. Cut the thread.

7 Wind the rest of the wool around the long side of the 6cm x 3cm card, 15 times.

8 Slip the wool off the card. Tie a length of wool around the centre in a knot.

9 Cut through the loops. Paste glue onto the middle of the strands where they are tied. Press the glued side onto the sock, just above the two buttons.

10 Glue a pom-pom onto the toe of the sock.

11 To work your puppet, slide your hand into the sock with your fingers between the wadding and the top of the card. Gently make the card fold along its crease (see step 3) to make a mouth. Slide your thumb under the folded card.

Hello. Do you want to hear my new joke?

Hand Puppet

With a little help from you, this hand puppet clown can shake hands, dance and do all sorts of other moves.

You will need:

* scissors
* polystyrene ball
* sheet of white tissue paper
* watered-down glue
* pale pink paint
* paintbrushes
* blue and red felt-tip pens
* 2 x 1m lengths of orange wool
* 2 x 10cm lengths of orange wool
* piece of card 7cm x 3cm   * glue
* circle of red T-shirt fabric (diameter 9cm)
* circle of yellow T-shirt fabric (diameter 35cm)
* 3 x 1.5cm pom-poms from a craft shop
* 2 small elastic hairbands

1 Using the scissors, carefully make a hole in the polystyrene ball large enough for your middle finger to fit inside.

2 Cover all of the ball except the hole with a layer of papier-mâché (see page 6). Use the watery glue and the tissue paper to do this. Mould a nose from the papier-mâché. Leave to dry. Paint the ball pale pink. Leave to dry.

3 Using the felt-tip pens, draw on a mouth, eyes and eyebrows.

4 Take one of the 1m lengths of orange wool. Wrap it around the piece of card.

5
Slip the wool off the card. Use one of the 10cm lengths of orange wool to tie it in the middle.

6
Cut through the loops. Repeat steps 4 and 5 with the other lengths of wool.

7
Paste glue onto the centre of the strands where they are tied. Stick the wool hair onto the side of the polystyrene ball. Repeat on the other side. Leave to dry.

8
Put a dab of glue onto the centre of the red circle of fabric. Place it glue side down in the middle of the yellow circle of fabric. Glue the three pom-poms onto the yellow fabric in a line. Leave to dry.

9
Put your middle finger under the centre of the red circle.

10
Push the polystyrene ball puppet head onto your finger on top of the fabric.

Slip a hairband over the fabric and your thumb.

Slip a second hairband onto the fabric and the finger next to your little finger.

Bring your puppet to life!

Hello. Time for some fun!

Kaleidoscope

Be dazzled when you watch the beads and sequins make magical patterns inside this great kaleidoscope.

You will need:

* a craft knife (ask an adult to use the knife)
* large cardboard crisp tube, its lid and the lid from a second tube the same size
* 3 strips of mirror board 62mm x 235mm
* masking tape
* compass and pencil
* yellow card
* pen * ruler
* scissors
* small beads, sparkly confetti and sequins
* sheet of wrapping paper
* circle of tracing paper 1cm larger than the diameter of the tube
* glue
* strips of thin orange card 1cm x 25cm

1 Take the plastic lid off the tube and leave it to one side. Ask an adult to cut off the bottom of the tube using the craft knife.

2 Tape the non-shiny side of the three strips of mirror board together.

3 With the shiny side on the inside, join the strips of mirror board together with masking tape to make a triangular prism.

4 Slot the mirror board shape into the tube so that its end is level with the cut end.

5 Open the compass to 9cm and use it to draw a circle on the yellow card. Cut out the circle.

6 Push the end of the pen into the centre hole made by the compass point. Push it through to make a bigger hole. Glue the card onto the cut end of the tube.

7 Carefully cut off the upright edge of one of the lids. Turn the cardboard tube upside down and press the circle of plastic into the end of the tube, so that it rests on top of the prism of mirror board.

8 Fill the space between the plastic circle and the top of the tube with the beads, confetti and sequins. Glue wrapping paper around the outside of the tube.

9 Lay the circle of tracing paper on top of the tube. Pop the lid back on to keep the tracing paper in place.

10 Take the strips of orange card. Glue them around the kaleidoscope as decoration.

Hold your kaleidoscope up to the light and look through the hole. Shake the kaleidoscope to make a different pattern.

How to Make a Pom-pom

Pom-poms are fun and easy to make. Turn them into pom-pom pets like the ones on pages 4 to 5 of this book. Or make smaller ones to fix onto hairbands or sew onto scarves or jumpers.

To make an 8cm pom-pom you will need:

* 2 pieces of card, 10cm x 10cm
* ruler
* compass and pencil
* scissors
* wool

1 Open the compass to 8cm using the ruler. Draw a circle on the card. Close the compass to 3cm. Keeping the point in the same place, draw a smaller circle. If you find it easier, trace the template on page 31 onto thin white paper. Cut it out. Trace around it onto the card.

2 Cut around the outer circle. Ask a grown-up to cut out the inner circle using sharp scissors. Now you have a card ring.

3 Repeat steps 1 and 2 to make a second card ring.

4 Put the card rings together. Cut several long pieces of wool. Take the first length of wool and wind it around and around the card rings, creating even layers. When the wool is too short to wind again, take another piece and repeat the process.

5 Keep winding the wool evenly until the hole in the centre is very small.

6 Slip the scissors between the card rings. Snip through the wool.

7 Tie a length of wool around the pom-pom, between the card rings. Knot the wool tightly. Tear off the card rings. Trim off any loose bits.

Templates

Dog ear

Pom-pom Pets
Pages 4 – 5

Cat ear

Dog ear

Dog muzzle

Cat ear

Dog nose

Cat muzzle

Cat nose

Monster Truck
Pages 12 – 13

Flames

Place on a fold

Puppet Theatre
Pages 18 – 19

Dolls' House
Pages 14 – 15

Target Board
Pages 16 – 17

30

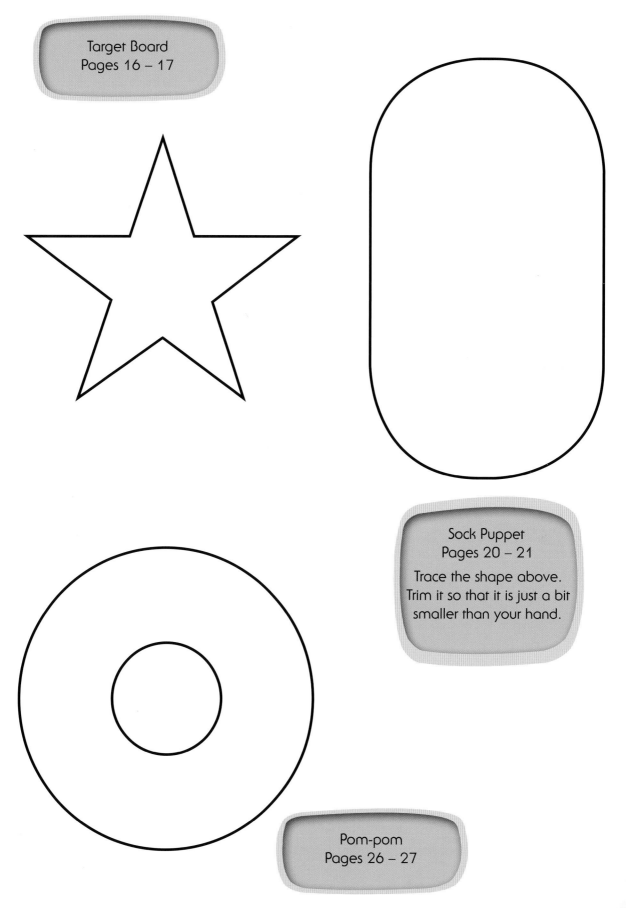

Target Board
Pages 16 – 17

Sock Puppet
Pages 20 – 21

Trace the shape above.
Trim it so that it is just a bit
smaller than your hand.

Pom-pom
Pages 26 – 27

Index

Further Information

Useful websites

The CBBC website has many craft, cooking and art activities that you might enjoy: www.bbc.co.uk/cbbc/thingstodo

Download templates to make historic toys at the Museum of Childhood, London's website: www.museumofchildhood.org.uk/learning/things-to-do's

Source craft supplies at: www.bakerross.co.uk/arts-and-crafts